San Jose Book Shop
1231-E Kentwood Avenue
San Jose, CA 95129
408-446-0590

Copyright © 1980
Marcus Books
195 Randolph Rd.
Toronto, Ontario
M4G 3S6

First printing September 1980
Second printing November 1980
Third printing May 1985

No part of this book may be reproduced in any form without the permission of the publishers.

All rights reserved.

Cover design by Art Gardner

Manufactured in Canada by Webcom Limited.

ISBN 0-919951-24-4

CONTENTS

Introduction	1
The Letter	3
Chapter 1: Life, Death and Spirit	5
Chapter 2: The Wheel of Rebirth	9
Chapter 3: The Power of Thought	11
Chapter 4: Illness and Aging	13
Chapter 5: The Agents of Disease	15
Chapter 6: The Inert Gases	19
Chapter 7: The Aquarian Age	23
Chapter 8: The Apocalypse	25
Chapter 9: Mind and the Subconscious	31
Chapter 10: Diet and Health	37
Chapter 11: Death, Immortality and the Astral Realms	43
Chapter 12: Symbolism, Sexuality and Love	49
Chapter 13: The Message	55

INTRODUCTION

This book is in the form of a letter to a thirteen-year-old girl, Michelle, written by a being from one of the higher spiritual planes. It was transmitted through me by a telepathic process which I developed a few years ago, and by which a total of four books in English have now been channelled through and published. These books form the 'Hilarion Series'.

The idea of using the form of a letter also originated with the source of the material. There is indeed a young girl by the name of Michelle who has actually had many of the experiences discussed in this text, however the real purpose of the book is to address those who are 'young' in a different sense than that of age: those who have yet to discover the magnificent and stimulating world of the spirit, but who know intuitively that there are realms of experience awaiting mankind which dwarf the purely mundane and practical existence that many believe to be the only reality.

This book is aimed at those who are dissatisfied with the life of distraction and constant anxiety that most people experience, and who are looking for a higher and more purposeful approach to existence. For them, this book offers a simple introduction to the ideas of the New Age, as it is called, and explains why the dawning of this New Age is not only necessary but inevitable. It will be a time of love and reunion among the human family, of peace and friendship among nations. From the midst of the gathering war clouds now upon the earth, such a vision may seem illusory. But as surely as the day follows the night, so must the dawning of the golden age of peace follow the horrors of the present night of war, destruction and upheaval.

I hope that some who read this book will be encouraged to change the patterns of despair, conflict and emptiness in their own lives or in the lives of those around them. Now is the time for the uplift of man. If we do not accomplish it from within ourselves, then we must perish from the earth.

May 1980.
Maurice B. Cooke
Toronto, Canada.

THRESHOLD
A letter for Michelle, from Hilarion

Dearest Michelle:

The time is at last ripe for us to explain to you, in a simplified way for now, some of the spiritual truths that you will have to understand if you are to attain all that you have set for yourself in this life. We have chosen this particular way, through your friend Mr. Cooke, knowing full well that the material so given would be made into a small book that many others could also read.

We have watched you grow in love and beauty, and we have seen how you have clung to the instinctive wisdom that your soul brought with it into this life. Do not slacken your grasp on this fountain of light, for it is a sure guide through all of the temptations that life will cast into your path. If you will only remember to stay true to the small inner voice within your heart's centre, then your footsteps will never go astray.

There are many children like yourself — children who have come to the earth voluntarily to be as beacons of love and wisdom for their brothers who no longer can see the truths of the spirit. Indeed, in this little book we wish to write down many of these truths in a simple way, not only for you, since you understand much already, but for the others as well — for those who have forgotten that they have come down to the earth level from a much higher place and are intended to return there.

In the chapters that follow, we will talk to you of many things as they are seen from our level. But it is up to you to seek your own grasp of these matters. The truth that is your truth is written in the scrolls of your heart, for that is where God lives. Teachers, guides and books can help, but only by awakening the knowledge that is already inside you.

Take what we offer you here, pass it through your own special magic of awareness and understanding, and then turn and give it out to others. Only remember that they too have their own particular point of view, and that you must never insist that your understanding is the only one that is right. God loves each human soul because it is different from the others, not because it is the same.

Finally, remember that you were created so that you could show God's own love in your treatment of all the living things that He has made. He is counting on the human race to achieve what other races in the galaxy have not wanted to try: to show what a permanent attitude of love, tolerance and brotherhood could do.

May you ever remember that your light is part of God's own light, that His love speaks always through your heart centre, and that your body was made to be a temple where His truth and goodness could forever dwell.

    With much Love,
    Hilarion

Chapter 1
Life, Death and Spirit

Do you remember that day in the woods, when you came upon the little dead bird by the side of the path? That was a sudden wrench for your young heart, because you did not understand how a creature which had been so alive could now be so motionless and still. It was an opportunity for you to learn one of the most important lessons that life has to teach, but you were then too young to grasp fully what the experience really meant.

You are older now, and approaching an age when the mystery of life and death can be understood. And yet, there is no mystery for the heart which realizes, as yours does, that physical bodies are merely as clothing that can be put on and taken off. The real life is not at the physical level, but at the level of spirit. The little bird which you found was not really the bird at all. It was just the discarded cloak that the *real* bird had left on the path. That real bird was still just as alive and vibrant as it had ever been, but your eyes were not quickened to the point where you could see him still flying joyously among the treetops.

The truth which awaits any who think carefully about life and death is simple: all of material manifestation — every physical body, every plant, tree, sun, or planet of the cosmos — is merely a *vehicle for learning,* an article of clothing that is put on for a time, and then discarded. But the being that goes through this experience of taking up and setting aside is spiritual, and you yourself are one of these spiritual beings.

You have come into this body to learn about yourself, for that is why any spiritual being takes on the cloak of matter. When you have learned what you can in this body, you will set it aside, just as you have set aside many others. Then you will pass to other levels and learn different things. But always your goal will remain the same: to *understand yourself*. That is the great task that is before every created spiritual being, and the purpose of any life — whether animal, plant, or cosmic — is to help in this important process of finding out about oneself.

What we would like you to understand is that everything you can see around you is merely the housing for a spiritual being whom your eyes cannot detect. You see only the outer cloak, not the inner essence. And yet you can see with your *heart*, if only you would allow yourself to look in this way. When you look with the heart, all of the spiritual realities lie open before you. It is your heart centre that tells you when someone is good, or selfish, or means to do you some injustice. Your heart can see what any person is really like, and its messages never lie.

We have said that your physical eyes do not see the spirit within, but there is a way to overcome this limitation: for the spiritual being who resides within every life-form in the animal category — including mankind — literally looks out from the pupils of the eyes. When you lock eyes with anyone, you feel instantly the close contact that this causes at the spiritual level. It is a reflection of the truth that the eyes are the windows of the soul.

Many people do not wish to look directly into the eyes of another. They fear the closeness of the contact. Sometimes they are afraid to allow another to see their real selves, for they know that there are dark patches there, and parts that could not stand the light of day. They will always avoid your gaze, through fear that you can read the truth.

But you yourself need never fear the scrutiny of another being. Your heart is pure and your soul if full of light. Let others see this loveliness, for there is all too little of it upon the earth now. You will find that your truth and goodness can lighten the burdens that others carry if you will only allow them to drink deep from the purity that smiles always from your beautiful eyes.

Chapter 2

The Wheel of Rebirth

In the first chapter we said that you had taken up the cloak of matter many times, and that implies that you have lived before on the earth. You yourself realize the truth of this statement, as do many people, for you can remember these past lives just below the level of your conscious thought. When you meet someone for the first time but feel you have known him for years, you are experiencing a memory of other lives. The fact that you cannot recall *details* of these other experiences is no proof that they did not exist. Even in *this* life it is hard to recall the details of things that happened to you a few years or even months ago.

The purpose of the wheel of rebirth, as it is called, is a simple one to understand. We have explained to you that the task that is before each spiritual being that comes down to take on a physical body is to try to understand itself more fully. If self-understanding can be improved, then the rough corners of the soul can be made smoother, and the things that are not settled in its make-up can be calmed. But this balancing and settling cannot be accomplished in a single life. Many experiences are needed on this earth before an individual can begin to round out all of his qualities, settle all the old problems, and come at last to a balanced view of himself, of creation, and of God.

We have mentioned old problems to be settled. Every soul who incarnates on the earth comes with many of these. For the most part they are problems with other *people* that have arisen in previous lives, through rivalry, through resentment or through fear. Whenever you allow yourself to feel an emotion like this against another person, you create a bond between you — one that must be untied one day because the bond is of the same nature as the emotion: rivalry creates bonds of contention; resentment creates bonds of dislike; and fear creates bonds of cowardice. These are not worthy ways in which to bind two people together. The only true bond in God's sight is that of love, for only love can release all the other, lesser ties, and only love can cement two souls together in a permanent union of growth and fulfillment.

There is more, much more, to the process of reincarnation, but what we have said here will give you the best introduction for now to the purposes behind the great cycle of rebirth, as it is experienced by individual souls.

Chapter 3

The Power of Thought

The bonds between souls which we spoke of in the last chapter are important for you to understand, for although they are not forged of physical matter (like chains or ropes), they are just as real and just as strong as if they were. The unseen forces that man creates with his mind are often even harder to control or escape from than the physical forces that he studies with his science.

Let us give you an example of this power of thought. Perhaps we should start to use the term *visualization,* for this is really what you do with your mind to create the forces that we are discussing. Imagine that a friend has a twelve-foot long plank which he lays down flat on the ground. He asks you to walk along it from one end to the other, and this you can do without difficulty. The plank is about one foot wide, and it is not hard to walk along it without falling off.

Now your friend takes the plank up to the top of two buildings that are fifteen stories tall. They are close together and he is able to set the plank so that it reaches across the space from one to the other. The distance is only ten feet, but under the plank are fifteen floors of empty space with a hard sidewalk at the bottom. He asks you again to walk along the plank. There is no wind, and the plank is quite solidly in place. Yet you cannot force yourself to walk along it, no matter how hard you *will* yourself to do it. The reason for this is your own ability to visualize: you see in your mind's eye what would happen if you slipped and fell, and this thought-picture is so strong that it prevents you from carrying out your friend's request, no matter how much you may wish to do so.

How strange that you could walk along the plank when it was on the ground, but not when it was fifteen stories high! Your balance and steadiness are the same — nothing has changed but the thought pictures in your head.

That is the proof that the power of *visualization* is far stronger than the power of man's *will*. In later chapters we will explain to you how to harness the tremendous power of your visualization ability, so that you can use it to smooth the pattern of your life, to acquire the skills you wish to have, and to gain the happiness that you deserve. It is a wonderful tool that God intended you to have and to use, for with it you can become a co-creator with Him, as you were meant to be.

Chapter 4

Illness and Aging

We have spoken to you about the ways in which bonds of resentment and fear can be created between two people by the power of thought. This power is responsible for terrible damage among mankind — not only in the relationships between individuals, but literally in its ability to cause illness and even death. And here we come upon one truth which, above all others, we wish to impress upon your mind. It is this: *what man suffers in terms of illness and physical deformity is only that which he himself has created by the power of his thought.*

In regard to illness of all kinds, there is an unseen but tremendously powerful process operating that literally allows an individual to make himself *physically* sick through the use of his mind. You may have heard someone say once that 'thoughts are things', and you might have wondered what it meant. That saying contains an important truth, because it is pointing out that the power of thought lies in its ability to *create something,* even though this creation is not at the level which you can see with your physical eyes. The level of this creation is what we call the *aetheric* level. The aether is a fine, invisible substance that is present throughout every part of your universe, even inside the atoms and molecules in what science thinks is merely 'empty space'. But space is not empty, because its very position with respect to higher worlds of creation is defined by the position of this subtle aether.

The most wondrous quality of this aether is its *response*

to thought. Whenever you imagine anything in your mind, the aether around you immediately takes up the picture and conforms to it in every detail. This process is quite beneficial so long as the thought being projected is a positive one. But many people on the earth now are in the habit of making only negative and harmful thoughts. They think ill of others, and they think ill of themselves. Is it any wonder that, eventually, they become literally ill?

The process can be explained more exactly: you have not only a physical body, but also a body made of this same aether which we have just described. The aether in your aetheric body is somewhat more compact than it is in the rest of space, but it is of the same material. This means that your aetheric body is also fully responsive to your thoughts. Whenever you imagine or 'see' yourself in a particular way, your aetheric body immediately *becomes that which you are visualizing*. When you stop holding the picture in your mind, the aetheric returns to normal — which is typically a close match to your physical body. If you think of yourself as beautiful, your aetheric vehicle becomes beautiful. If you think of yourself as old and haggard, the same conformity comes about. The tragedy is that many people on this earth habitually picture themselves as old, because of their *fear* of growing old. They are so afraid of aging and losing their attractiveness that they concentrate all of their powerful visualization ability on this picture that they fear. Instantly, whenever this picture of age comes into their mind, their aetheric body *becomes old*. And because the physical body is so closely connected with the aetheric body, a repeated picture of aging will affect not only the aetheric, but eventually the physical body as well. Literally, these people are *thinking themselves old* — through fear.

This is all that needs to be said for now in relation to thought and its ability to bring general changes to the body. In the next chapter we will explain how another kind of projection causes the acute and chronic illnesses which attack particular parts of the body.

Chapter 5

The Agents of Disease

In this chapter we will try to explain to you how thought fuelled by *emotion* brings about acute and chronic illness. We have already pointed out the way in which the aetheric body reacts to thought — by instantly conforming itself to any picture of it that the mind projects. But there are ways of creating aetheric forms, which we call *thought-forms,* that no one is fully aware of: this process involves *negative emotion.* Whenever an individual is in the grip of any emotion, he creates a specific aetheric form or *thought-form* which has the same basic nature as the emotion. If the emotion is that of resentment, the thought-form is of a certain quality. If the emotion is fear, or greed, or worry, or whatever, the thought-form is always of a matching quality or vibration. Now, the human body has many different organs and systems in it, each one having a different basic quality or vibration. When a person projects an emotional thought-form of a negative kind, that thought-form is automatically attracted to a particular part or organ of the individual's body which is closest in vibration to the thought-form. The form then goes to that part, settles there, and (if it can) begins to alter the function or the structure of that body part to suit itself. The details of the process are quite complex, and cannot be explained to you now, but we think that the description above will be clear to your understanding.

Let us try to illustrate this process by using an example from your own life. A few months ago you came down with mononucleosis. This disease is one which is caused by a thought-form that many young people project, through the emotion of being 'tired of doing something'. Often it is school work that they are 'tired' of, but regardless of where this emotion is focussed, the ideas of lassitude and tiredness are present. Now, the bodily system that is closest in quality to 'tiredness' is the lymph system, which includes the spleen, the lymph passages and nodes, and the tonsils. This is because the lymph system is the 'laziest' system of the body. It depends on other systems to act as its pump — whether muscular, blood or respiratory. Therefore it is natural for the mononucleosis thought-form to attack the lymph system, as it did in your own case. We know you remember how sore your stomach was when the thought-form was mainly located in your spleen. The pain came when the thought-form had managed to make the spleen very inflamed and swollen. Your body's natural defenses forced the thought-form up to the tonsils, and the result of that was your sore throat. Finally, when your friend Mr. Cooke came to see you, the energy beams from his inert gas apparatus caused the thought-form to be literally disintegrated, and this is why you felt much better within a few days of his treatment.

Unfortunately, you were still feeling 'tired' of certain things in your life, and therefore you re-created a partial thought-form similar to the one that had been destroyed. That is why it took you a little longer to be fully cured.

Many doctors believe that this form of mononucleosis is infectious; that is, that it can be transmitted from one person to another. In a sense they are right, but they do not fully understand the mechanism of the transfer between two persons. The transfer takes place strictly at the aetheric level, since that is the level at which the thought-form exists. But the person who 'picks it up' from the other can only do so if he already has a tendency in the same direction. In other words, he must also have an attitude of being 'tired' of something in his life, before the mononucleosis thought-form can really take hold of his lymph system.

The final proof that mononucleosis is connected with the thought of being 'tired' of something is the way it first made you feel. Like everyone who is attacked by this disease, all you wanted to do at first was sleep. This is an example of how the symptoms of a disease can be used as a clue to the nature of the thought that creates it.

In the next chapter we will explain more about the marvellous properties of the energy fields which Mr. Cooke used to help you on your way to recovery.

Chapter 6

The Inert Gases

There are many wonderful ways to use the material world around you for your benefit. Science has discovered only a small percentage of these up to now — partly because of man's limited imaginative ability, and partly because some of these special technologies could not be allowed to fall into his hands so long as he continued to make war on himself. Let us discuss both of these limitations separately.

The inability to accept a particular thing as being possible is the surest way of ensuring that it will never be acheived. This is a truth of such paramount importance that we could not possibly stress it too greatly. When any person decides that such-and-such is impossible, he sets up an energy pattern in his life that ensures he will never experience it. For example, many people are convinced that their eyes can see only at the 'physical' level, and they pass off as pure fantasy the claims of some individuals who are able to see auras and other lights around human bodies. Those who dismiss these gifts are making certain that *they* will never develop them.

It is the same with scientific development. A scientist who does not believe in perpetual motion, or in the possibility of obtaining energy without having to burn up some other form of energy, is ensuring that *he* will never be able to discover them. His mind has dismissed the possibility, and this closes the door to finding it.

Many attempts have been made to enlarge the horizons of possibility that man's mind can contemplate. The various 'space' movies have been particularly helpful in this task, beginning with the television series, *Star Trek*. All of these efforts at broadening man's mind have been strongly overshadowed by higher beings who know that unless the human race can allow itself to imagine a better world, a more advanced world in spiritual and technical terms, then such a world can literally never be attained.

The inert gas energy beams developed by your friend Mr. Cooke, using information we have given to him, are a good example of a new technology that does not conform to the 'laws of science' as man now understands them. It is for this reason that scientifically trained individuals have such difficulty in accepting the idea that the inert gases could possibly have the wonderful characteristics demonstrated by Mr. Cooke and his associates. The special ability of these gases, when pressurized and placed in a magnetic field, to give off energy of a subtle nature without ever needing to be 'charged up' or without 'running down', is the stumbling block that prevents many scientists from accepting that the gases can act in this way. However, as you yourself found out, these energy fields really do exist and have a wonderful capacity to drive out thought-forms of the kind that cause illness. In your own case, Mr. Cooke used the gas Argon to generate a strong field at a location just above your head, and this field was very antagonistic to the mononucleosis thought-form that had invaded your lymph system. After about thirty minutes of exposure to this energy, that thought-form could not remain in your body and voluntarily left. That is why, after about two days of allowing your body to rid itself of many accumulated poisons, you began to feel much better. Your friend has delved into several other possible uses for these gases, including their ability to relieve migraine headaches and to regrow body tissues that have deteriorated. We do not wish to discuss the details of this new technology any further in this book because our purpose here is merely to sketch briefly a large number of the ideas that will form the structure of the New Age. In the next chapter of this book, we will talk more about this New Age, and what it means in your own life.

Earlier in this chapter we said that man had not been allowed to develop certain of the more advanced technologies because he had not yet learned to live in peace. It has been the responsibility of 'observers', who have come here from other parts of this galaxy, to limit such technological knowledge. These observers have other functions as well, one of which is to come to man's aid when the chaos of the current phase of life on the earth increases to a dangerous point. Another reason for their presence is the need to monitor man's use — or misuse — of nuclear energy. These observers know things about nuclear energy that man does not, and they know the extreme danger of an uncontrolled chain reaction taking place at certain high-energy locations on the earth. In most cases these high-energy points are at the geographic locations of large cities, and unfortunately the most likely targets for nuclear bombing in the coming war are these very same cities. The danger is simply that the chain reaction of the explosive power may not confine itself to the radioactive material in the bomb, but might well spread to other material around the point of the explosion — *material that is not radioactive*. This would cause an explosion so powerful that a large fragment of the earth could be blown away, and the very fabric of space itself could be torn. The fact is that at these locations of high energy on the earth's surface, the threshold of explosive power needed to start a chain reaction in normal, non-radioactive material is much lower than in other places.

You will now understand better the other main reason why the observers are patrolling the earth: they wish to be in a position to halt any nuclear explosion which threatens to start a spreading chain reaction into other material around the bomb itself. The observers are fully capable of this kind of control, through their very advanced technology, but they need to monitor the earth *constantly* in order that nothing will get started without their knowledge.

We did not mean to frighten you with the ideas presented in this chapter. Indeed, you yourself need never fear for your own safety or that of your loved ones. But we wanted to take this opportunity to explain the realities behind man's dangerous toying with nuclear power, so that others who read this book will see in their minds the abyss that the race is standing beside, and the dedication of the galactic helpers who wish to protect humanity from itself.

Chapter 7

The Aquarian Age

In the last chapter we mentioned briefly that a New Age was coming soon upon this planet, and in this chapter we would like to explain that concept more fully.

Look about you at the life that many people lead today. It is a pattern of stress, self-indulgence, irritation and a deep dissatisfaction with what existence offers in return for all the effort put into it. Is it any wonder that many souls are afflicted in the mind, or that there is so much illness, early aging and premature death, or that many think life itself is without any purpose or meaning?

Part of the reason for the spread of this empty life-style is the hold which the *Piscean* energies have had on mankind over the last two thousand years. The earth stands now at the gateway into the next age (for each one lasts about 2,000 years), and if you are going to make the transition smoothly into this wonderful new time on the earth, it is important for you to understand fully what both the old age and the new one stand for, and to appreciate why the change-over period now being experienced is so chaotic and threatening.

Let us look first at the Piscean energies that have governed the period now coming to a close. In the ancient science of Astrology, it is understood that each of the great ages upon the earth is given to a different zodiac sign, and that the basic qualities of that sign will greatly influence the general trends of events during the age. The nature of Pisces is best summed up in the word *sorrow*. If you come to study in detail the history of the time since the Master

Jesus walked the earth, you will readily see that sorrow has indeed characterized much of man's experience. In no earlier time have men been so heartlessly cruel to their brothers. Never before has humanity waged such devastating war and slaughter upon itself. Even in 'civilized' countries of the present day, inner sorrow and desperation are found on every hand.

Pisces is also the zodiac sign which represents illusion and self-deception. Its planetary ruler is Neptune, god of the sea, and you can easily understand that the sea image is a good one to suggest illusion or 'things not being what they seem'. If you have ever tried to open your eyes underwater, you will know how distorted and hazy everything appears.

In the age of Pisces, man deluded himself in many ways. He thought that he could get along without God or a concept of the Creator. Atheism and insanity were the result. He thought he could use whatever he found in the earth's crust for as long as he liked. The depletion of natural resources was the result. And worst of all, he thought it was acceptable to harbor hatred and rivalry against other groups and peoples. And world war was the result.

Now it is time for mankind to open its eyes in the clear light of reality and to see at last that there is only one way for men to live together: in harmony, brotherhood and love. That is the keynote of the Aquarian Age, and if man cannot grasp the truth of this statement, then there is little hope for him. It is impossible — and will not be permitted — for humanity to continue on the downward path to self-destruction which it is now treading. During the coming years, it is expected that millions will find a better approach to life and will learn to give up all the destructive habits of action and thought which have afflicted their lives. When this happens, the New Age will literally dawn in their hearts. And when enough men come to this awakening of the Aquarian ideal of brotherhood and love, it will actually dawn upon the whole earth.

Chapter 8

The Apocalypse

You have heard much about a 'time of trouble' for the earth. The thought-form of the *Apocalypse* is now hovering over the entire planet, and all who are sensitive to the vibrations of thought can tap into it. This is a different kind of thought-form from that which we discussed in our earlier chapter on illness. Nonetheless it is a thought-form all the same, and it has an equal power to cause a reaction in individuals. It is not the reaction of illness, but one of attitude and expectation.

Millions of human beings are aware that a very difficult time is about to descend upon the earth. In most cases they are aware only at the subconscious level. This is why so many are drawn to books and films that deal with the ideas of universal destruction and ultimate evil. They do not know why they should be so fascinated with these concepts, for at the conscious level they do not understand the nature of the times through which they are living. But the subconscious recognition, in these films and books, of the very scenarios which are planned for the earth in the next few years draws them irresistibly.

In a few cases, individuals know at the *conscious* level what is in store. These people are generally those who have remained aware of the higher truths and who have deliberately sought to understand the nature of the period through which the race is living. This series of books, for example, has been prepared specifically for those who want to understand earlier than the others the meaning of the chaos toward which humanity is heading.

We will try to explain to you in simple terms the reasons which make such a time of trouble inevitable. The main point to be made is that, without such a period of difficulty and testing, the race of man literally *would not be able to advance to the next rung on the ladder of progress*.

But many more particular goals are also to be achieved through this troubled phase of history. Firstly, there is an absolute necessity that the immense thought-form of hatred and bigotry which man's thoughts have cast over the whole earth be removed. Again, this thought-form is not of the same nature as those which cause physical illness. It results in an illness to be sure, but it is an illness of the soul.

This sort of thought-form is made by man's own thoughts, and it is dissipated by man's actions. That idea is very important, and we will try to explain it more clearly for you.

Whenever you think a powerful negative thought, a negative thought-form is created. Whenever you *do* the action which the thought suggests, you sap the strength of the thought-form and it dissapears. Suppose you become extremely angry with someone, and you *think* about hitting that person. But you don't actually do it. This will create a thought-form around you which is of the same nature as the thought itself: one of physical violence toward someone else. Now, if you do not actually carry out the action corresponding to the thought, the thought-form will remain at the aetheric level. From that level it will *try* to manifest. It does this by seeking to make you do some act of violence which is similar to its own essence. If you give in to the pressure of the thought-form and indulge in some violent act, the 'substance' of the thought-form literally feeds into the muscles that are involved in the violent act, and this causes the thought-form to disappear.

It is the same with the gigantic thought-form of hatred and bigotry which the race as a whole has made and which hovers in the space surrounding this planet. Over the past decades, there has been more hateful and bigoted *thought* than there has been *action*, and this means that the thought-form has continually increased in power. The 'action' to which this thought-form corresponds is that of warfare and violence between groups, and such action is the only one which is capable of getting rid of this horrible cancer that sprawls upon the living earth.

So you can see that, in a sense, it is *necessary* for there to be some form of conflict on a large scale in order that the earth can be cleansed of this thought-form. This may sound as if we are saying that the war would be a good thing. Nothing could be further from our meaning. What we are saying is this: that is is *man* who has created the conditions which are inevitably drawing the race into global conflict, and that even though that conflict will be a terrible ordeal for the race, it will have at least the benefit of dissipating the dreadful thought-form of hatred and contempt which the thoughts of millions of men have created.

But other positive ends will also be achieved by this time of war and difficulty. One of these is to demonstrate in unmistakable terms the nature of the habits which the race has adopted. We are referring to habits of irritation, rivalry, aggression, bigotry and so forth. We have said to you already that one of the reasons for any spiritual being coming into the material plane and taking on a physical body, is to allow it to see itself clearly, and to *understand itself*. In many ways, reality at your level is like a mirror, reflecting back to every soul the true nature of itself. The circumstances in the life of any individual accurately reflect various facets of that individual's nature, and by coming into a life which will conform itself to that inner pattern, the individual is allowed to see *outside* himself certain truths that relate to what is *inside*. For example, a man who marries a woman and who then proceeds to experience conflict constantly with her, is merely living through a pattern which reflects some quality *within him-*

self. The marriage which he has made is like a stage on which his own internal conflicts can be acted out. By going through this acting out of conflict, his inner problem can be seen more clearly. Often the 'seeing' is not at the conscious but at the subconscious level — but either way, the lesson is learned.

Now, in the case of mankind as a whole, there is a necessity that the internal characteristics of rage, hatred, rivalry and aggression be recognized, for unless this can be done, there will be no incentive for the race to change. This is where the reality-mirror comes in. When millions of human beings begin to experience, in hard reality, the results of the thought-form of hatred and aggression, they will be able to understand better than ever before that *they do in fact have these flaws*. Man spends billions of dollars on 'defense', or so it is called. He tells himself that he must do so, because the other side is also spending huge sums on armaments. But the result of all of this thought-power expended in designing and fabricating weapons of destruction *must* eventually manifest. And in so doing, it will show to all who experience it the true nature of their thought. When guns are made, guns will be used. When bombs are made, bombs will be used. The energy put into the manufacture of these things *requires* this to happen.

And yet this law which inevitably pulls thought down into manifestation is intended for man's benefit and salvation. Without this process, man would never become aware of the things he harbors inside him, and he would never be moved to purify himself of his negativity.

Another purpose for this time of upheaval on the earth relates to the great Law of Karma as it affects humanity. This law is also known as the law of Cause and Effect. You know about this concept as it relates to physical science, for you have studied it in school. When you mix two given materials, a specific reaction occurs. Whenever the same two materials are brought together, the same result is noted. Another example is in relation to illness, as we have explained to you in an earlier chapter. When an individual creates a thought-form of the kind that produces disease, it will inevitably invade his own body and produce the symptoms to which it corresponds. Both of these examples are part of the working of karma, broadly understood.

But this great law has applications which go far beyond the simple examples we have just given. Its most important activity in terms of the human race has to do with the karmic patterns that each individual brings over with him from his past lives. The Law of Karma requires that any action an individual takes remains forever with him, as if that action were frozen or 'stuck' to that individual. This idea of 'adhering' action goes beyond the actual life in which the action was done, unless in that life the individual has been able to cancel out the action by *living through its effect*. If the action was one of love or helpfulness, then there is no need to be rid of the consequence of that action. It remains ever with the person as a halo of help and spirituality. But when the action was against the Creator's laws and brought pain or distress to any living creature, then the nature of the adhering 'stuff' is very negative and hindering in terms of the advancement of the soul. This 'stuff' which each action generates is not the same as a thought-form. It is a more subtle material, which is able to exist apart from your three-dimensional world. This is why it can come again and again into incarnation along with the incarnating soul. And this is also why it must some day be cancelled out — if it is of the negative kind.

God has allowed a process by which the negative karma accumulated as a result of harmful actions can be removed. This comes about when the individual who was responsible for the action goes through the equivalent experience of pain *himself*. For example, if you have caused another person to feel emotional pain by saying hurtful things to him, the normal way to get rid of the negative karma which comes from that action is to have someone else say similar things to you at some later point. This point can be in the same life, or in a later one. The timing of the meeting with your karma does not matter. What is important is that, at some time, all of your negative karma must be met and cancelled out. For most people, there still remains a great deal of negative karma to be dealt with, and another purpose of the time of trouble currently descending upon the earth is to allow them to lift from their own shoulders most of the karma with which they still must deal.

You may have wondered, in looking about you at the world, why you should have been so lucky as to have been born in a safe and plentiful country, while millions of other human beings have apparently had the ill luck to be born into conditions of poverty, illness and war.

It has nothing to do with luck. Every soul is born into just the right circumstances to allow him to set aside a large part of the karmic burden he carries. Many have been responsible for such a great amount of pain in others that they can only hope to set the resulting karma aside if they are subjected to what may appear to be very cruel circumstances. Yet, for such souls, a life of this kind is *literally the only chance.* A life lived in a free and peaceful country would have left them no further ahead in terms of setting aside their karmic burden. And unless the burden can be discharged, they will not be able to advance along with the rest of humanity when it moves forward into the spirituality and light of the Aquarian Age.

That is all we wish to say about this time of upheaval for now.

Chapter 9

Mind and the Subconscious

We now wish to speak about the nature of the mind. There is a general understanding among mankind that the mind consists of the conscious part, and a larger portion which has been called the unconscious, or *sub*conscious. To a large degree this breakdown corresponds to reality but it is not as complete as might be hoped. We will try here to set out a correct understanding of the various parts of the mind of man, in the hopes that certain factors of behaviour and thought among the human family can be better understood.

The conscious mind can be compared to the tip of an iceberg — the portion that projects *above* the level of the water. The unconscious is like the part which lies submerged, which is many times larger than the conscious or projecting part. The water, in this comparison, is like the sea of universal thought, or what a well-known author has called the *collective unconscious*. The collective unconscious is like a sea of 'mind-stuff' into which all of the individual minds of the human race can tap. But in reality, this sea of mind is the sea of spirit. What most people do not understand is that the mind — the mental capacity to reason and think — is the closest thing that physical man has to pure spirit. This all-pervading sea of spiritual material extends vastly beyond the limit of your own three-dimensional space, and is not confined to it. Indeed, your mental powers are among the highest qualities you have, in spiritual terms, and will remain a part of you for almost all of your later journey into the higher realms —

after you have ceased to need the experience of rebirth into the physical or earth-plane. (Finally, even that quality will be transcended, but this book cannot teach you about that distant goal.)

Let us go back to the comparison involving the iceberg. The tip that protrudes above the water is solidly connected with the other, deeper portion. In the same manner, your conscious mind is connected with a large part of your thinking capacity of which you are not normally aware. This larger part or subconscious is in many ways like a computer which can store information and can solve problems of a straight-forward kind. It also has the ability to repeat over and over again what it picks up from the conscious mind. The important thing to remember about the subconscious part of your mind is that it is the *follower* and not the leader. It always takes its cue from the conscious mind. There is however a process at work in many people which allows the subconscious repeating ability to greatly influence the thoughts in the conscious mind, in a way that produces much damage, and even physical illness.

Let us explore this concept further. Do you remember when you were younger how much fun it was to pick up the little rhymes and verses your mother used to read to you and then say them over and over? Perhaps you can even recall the thrill of discovering *rhyme itself*. Many adults are so many years away from their childhood that they have forgotten this wonderful discovery that some words sound like others; but to a young child coming upon it for the first time, it is very exciting. The reason why it is so delightful is because it represents the first real awakening of the dormant subconscious in the child. Until that discovery, the subconscious has little input into the conscious mind, and merely collects data and memories. But the discovery of rhyme brings the subconscious into its own element. For the major job of the subconscious is to help you to *remember,* and remembering is always easier if there is a rhyme involved.

Now, another important factor in the operation of the subconscious is the idea of *repetition*. Even without the help of a rhyme, the subconscious can recall things better when those things are repeated to it. This is why, in many teaching systems for children, the use of repetition is so stressed. It was realized that a child will remember something if he repeats it to himself a sufficient number of times.

That is an extremely important concept because this very advantage in terms of school learning becomes a decided *dis*advantage in cases of emotional stress where the person, as a child, has been told things repeatedly that have made him think *badly* of himself.

The damage is almost always the fault of the parents. Many parents think that the only way to make a child good is to tell him that he is 'bad', or at least to stress the times when he has displeased them but to say nothing when he has been good. If the parents never tell the child that he is good, and only point out the times when he is bad, then the child will get the message at the subconscious level *that he is only bad*.

The worst damage is done when the experience of negative criticism happens repeatedly. If the damaging statements are a repeating pattern in the child's life, then they will become literally a repeating pattern in the child's subconscious. In exactly the same way that the child learns the multiplication table, he also learns to accept subconsciously what his parents tell him — either by word or by *deed*. This idea of *action* being the teacher is also extremely important. If, for example, a child is not made to feel loved through the actions of the parents, the pain and loneliness within the child will also become a repeating pattern in the child's subconscious, and this will tend to repeat endlessly to him like a broken record.

You might think that you do not hear with the conscious mind what the subconscious mind is repeating to itself, but this is not true. The conscious always hears, although it often refuses to pay attention. But in off-guard moments, the subconscious messages are listened to carefully by the conscious mind, as when you are daydreaming or falling asleep. Do you ever wonder where those song-fragments come from that you can't seem to stop in your ear? It is simply your subconscious humming to itself.

Now, the damage done by implanting these harmful ideas into the subconscious can be *corrected,* if one only knows how to go about it. The easiest way to do this is, firstly, to recognize precisely the nature of the damaging thought that the subconscious is repeating to itself, and then to start a program of positive affirmation in which the *opposite* of the harmful thought is forced into the subconscious. By doing this, the subconscious can be persuaded to repeat helpful and positive things, rather than harmful and discouraging things. The most successful way to approach such a project is to utilize *rhyme.* Once you have discovered the nature of the thought that you wish to change, you can devise two lines of rhyming verse which say the thing you want to substitute into your subconscious repeating pattern.

For example, suppose that you were made to feel, when you were younger, that you would never really be a beautiful woman, and that you had certain disadvantages of feature that would doom you to being plain all your life. Now, in the first place, such a notion is ridiculous since you are already one of the most lovely of souls upon the earth, and it is the *soul* that determines whether others find you physically beautiful or not. But merely for us to tell you that you are beautiful will do no good, *so long as you do not believe it yourself.* Therefore, for your own peace of mind and happiness, it is important for you to retrain your subconscious so that it will tell you good things about the way you look, rather than things that suggest that you are not beautiful. Simply make up a rhyme which tells you in straightforward terms that you are beautiful, charming or whatever you wish yourself to be. Repeat that rhyme to yourself twenty times before you go to sleep at night, and twenty times again upon awakening. After a week of that schedule, your subconscious will start to parrot the same thought back to your conscious mind, and when that starts, you won't have to continue with the conscious affirmation. If this procedure could be adopted by mankind generally, then much stress, pain, doubt, and shame could be avoided.

To continue along this line of thought: in the fourth chapter of this book, we explained how the aetheric body responds to the thought-pictures which the visualizing ability projects. The subconscious also plays a part in this procedure, for if the thought or picture is projected *repeatedly* by the conscious mind, the subconscious will eventually pick up the pattern and continue it *ad infinitum*. Now, if the picture is one of aging, and if this thought is repeated often enough, the subconscious will adopt it and the result will be that the aetheric body becomes and *remains* permanently old. When this takes place, it is just a matter of time before the physical body conforms itself to the aetheric pattern.

What we have just explained is literally the *cause* of aging and the decay of the physical body in as much as half of the human family now on the earth. The aging process in the remainder is more complex and involves questions of diet and the entertaining of harmful emotional states on an almost permanent basis. We have already explained how emotion of a negative kind generates harmful thought-forms, and how these aetheric energies cause damage to the physical body. What we have not yet explained is how certain kinds of food also cause aging and early death to the human body. We will deal with that topic in the next chapter.

Chapter 10

Diet and Health

The food that passes through your body is of the utmost importance for your health, your mental balance and your emotional well-being. When you eat any given food, you are not merely eating the molecules and atoms in that food. You are also eating the astral and the aetheric counterparts. If the astral part is full of poisons, then these will lodge in your own astral body. If the aetheric body is contaminated, your aetheric body will likewise be adversely affected.

We have just introduced a new concept to you — namely, the idea of the astral body — and we wish to take a short space to explain to you more fully what that is. You know that you have a physical and an aetheric body. The physical is the seat of the physical sensations and pleasures, whereas the aetheric responds primarily to thought. Even where the thoughts are fuelled by emotion, it is nonetheless the *thought* that forms the aether into a pattern that reflects the thought. But for the emotions by themselves, there is also a separate body. This is the astral body, which is the seat of the emotions that you feel, and which is very strongly affected by these emotions. Any emotion other than love or friendship tends to weaken the astral body, and those who allow emotions like hatred, resentment, fear or worry to take them over are doing untold damage to the beautiful astral body that they have been given. This is a point of extreme importance, because the astral body is the body in which each person finds himself after he has died and left his physical vehicle. This means that those who harbor damaging emotions on a continuing basis end up with a weak or crippled astral body, and they must inhabit this damaged vehicle after they have died.

Consider first that there are two basic categories of food which mankind eats at present: animal and vegetable. In the first category are included meat, eggs, milk and other dairy products. The second category includes all the fruits, grains and vegetables that are known.

When a fruit is picked, or when a vegetable is pulled from the plant or the ground, there is, in a sense, a certain resistance 'felt' by the fruit or vegetable. This resistance is a kind of emotion, but it is so different from the emotions of mankind in vibration and in strength, that the slight contamination which occurs in the *astral* body of the fruit or vegetable does not noticeably harm the astral body of the human being who consumes it. But the astral body of an *animal* who is killed picks up a very *large* quantity of negative emotion that acts like a poison to the animal and, of course, to the human who consumes the flesh of that animal. The poison comes from the *fear* which the animal feels prior to its death. Many people think that a cow or a lamb does not know it is being taken to the slaughterhouse and to its death, but this is not so. The animals are extremely precognitive, and they know very well when they are being taken to die. This arouses much fear and desperation within them, and the result is the contamination firstly of their own astral bodies, and secondly of the astral body of any person who eats the flesh of the slain animals.

After years of consuming large quantities of meat that contains this astral poison, the human body starts to deteriorate. This is due to a prior deterioration and wasting of the astral body of that human being. ultimately, the physical body starts to conform to the infirmities of the astral body, and both aging and early death are the result. By 'early death', we mean death at a date earlier than would have occurred in the absence of these poisons.

There is an expression many people are familiar with, namely that 'man is what he eats'. What is not so well understood is that, if man is what he eats, then surely the eating of death in the form of flesh must bring death itself closer. That is precisely what takes place, as we have now explained.

In an earlier chapter, we dealt with the concept of karma. You can perhaps appreciate that by causing pain and fear in the animals that are slaughtered for food, a large quantity of karma is placed upon the human race as a whole. This is shared by all humans to varying degrees, but those who eat meat take on much more than those who do not, and those who actually raise the animals for food, or operate the slaughterhouses where they are killed, have an enormous burden of karmic debt to discharge.

In the case of someone who merely eats the meat but who does not participate further in the carnage, the karma is usually set aside through the episodes of illness which most people undergo, and which are promoted by the very weakness that the eating of the meat causes. There are, of course, certain meat-eaters who appear never to become ill, this being due to a very strong metabolism which they have inherited genetically. In such cases, the karma from the meat-eating is inevitably to be met through undergoing death at an earlier age than would have been the case had no meat been eaten.

The interesting fact regarding the damage that is gradually done to the astral body through the continual eating of meat is that if the meat-eating is stopped for a period of nine months, the astral body will be able to restore itself to a near perfect state. Its regenerative powers are remarkable so long as it is not being continually weakened by the consumption of the astral poison generated by the fear that the animal experienced before it was killed.

You can now understand that there are basically only three things that can make you ill: what you think, what you feel, and what you eat. All a man needs is a happy mind, a loving heart and a pure diet in order to remain at the peak of health until the end of his days. Unfortunately, the harmful habits of many people are so ingrained that they cannot be expected to change them overnight, even were they persuaded of the wisdom of doing do. The underlying purpose of this book is to convince many that they *should* think about changing their habits of thought, emotion and diet, since they stand only to gain by any change which makes their minds happier, their hearts more loving, and their food more pure.

The last point we wish to make about the question of meat-eating relates to the difference between warm-blooded animals and cold-blooded ones. The significance of warm blood is that it corresponds to a relatively well-developed emotional nature. Thus is is that cows, lambs and pigs have a more sensitive emotional nature than fish, for example, which are cold-blooded creatures. Indeed, since fish are cold-blooded, their astral bodies are not close in vibration to that of mankind, and therefore the astral poisons which are generated in the fish's astral are not very damaging to the astral of man. There is some contamination of course, but the degree is considerably less.

Any person who wishes to alter his diet in the direction here suggested would do well firstly to drop red meat and switch to fish (and fowl — also a white meat). This can be continued for about four to six months while gradually replacing the fish/fowl content of the diet with dairy sources of protein: eggs, cheese, milk and the like. After a period of eight months or so, the person may notice that he does not want to eat as much protein as before — that the consumption of protein gives him a 'full' feeling, as if he had eaten too much. This is a signal from the body that the amount of protein being consumed can be reduced.

What many people do not realize is that their need for protein is largely due to *habit*. The body (specifically the liver) is quite capable of recycling virtually *all* of the body's protein without requiring an additional supplement from outside, but most people have developed a *habit* of protein-eating which has caused the liver to become lazy so that it no longer works at recycling the body's own protein. It knows that a large quantity of additional 'outside' protein will be given to it on a daily or weekly basis, and it does not wish to expend energy on a task (recycling protein) that is not necessary to survival.

As this recycling ability re-awakens, the person trying to modify his diet will find that periodic fasts can speed along the process of change. When the body fasts, many alterations in the metabolism can be effected more quickly, and a 'leap forward' in terms of diet change can be accomplished in a relatively short time. The best form of fast is one in which either juice or whole juicy fruit is taken, but no protein or oil sources. Also whole vegetables should be avoided while fasting. There are many excellent books on the process of fasting, and we recommend those by Airola as a good introduction to the essential ideas.

We want to mention only one more factor in regard to the question of eating meat. This has to do with the concept of the earth-plane as a mirror for one's own inner states — an idea we have already explained to you. Now, if the world outside is programmed, so to speak, to reflect the inner states of humanity, is it not clear that as long as man continues to put death *inside* him, (by eating the cadavers of animals), he will never be able to stop the death and killing that is going on *around* him? This universal law of reflection makes it inevitable that the slaughter of animals and the slaughter of human beings will continue together, and that the one cannot be stopped unless the other is also stopped.

We have given you all we can on the subject of diet. In the next chapter we will turn our attention to the fascinating subject of death — fascinating because it is a total *illusion* in all senses of the word.

Chapter 11

Death, Immortality, and the Astral Realms

The question of death has confused and frightened mankind ever since the process of discarding the physical body began. This process, however, is not one that has always been used by the human race. There was a time when no death occurred, and all those who had been put on the earth in the beginning simply remained alive through a regenerative procedure that allowed the body to repair worn tissue on a continuing basis. That constant repair of tissue is now impossible, for two reasons. The first is the near-absence of a certain gaseous constituent in the atmosphere: Xenon. The second has to do with man's thoughts and emotions. Even if the amount of Xenon in the atmosphere were returned to the level at which it existed in the period prior to the beginning of the death experience, the damage self-inflicted by mankind through negative thought and emotion would overcome the regenerative help available from the gas Xenon, and men would continue to die.

We wish to touch briefly upon the quality of the gas Xenon which allows it to prompt the body to regenerate all worn tissue on a continuing basis. In an earlier chapter we stated that the inert gases (which include Xenon) could be raised to a state of excitation through the use of pressure and a magnetic field. In this excited state, the inert gases are able to generate energy beams which can have remarkable effects in the medical sense. You have already benefited from the use of one of these gases.

For Xenon, however, there is a special property in the

generated field which allows a body exposed to it to tap into the available energy so that it can rebuild tissue of all kinds. The field itself does not contain the pattern on which the tissue is reconstructed. The body is able to use its astral counterpart as a model for any rebuilding task, even the growth of new fingers or new limbs. But in the present low energy state surrounding the earth, the body does not have any extra source of power that it can use for this kind of project, and so does not attempt any major reconstructions of itself. If the atmosphere were to contain again the high level of Xenon which was there about three million years ago, the human race could use the generated energy just as it did then. If, in addition, all negative thought and emotion could be eradicated, death would again become a rare occurrence. This idea will sound fantastical to most who read this book, but we assure you that it is literally possible for the body to regenerate all of its tissue on a continuing basis, given a sufficient level of Xenon energy, and given the absence of harmful thought and emotion. The Xenon needs merely to be under some pressure and within a magnetic field for it to produce its energy. Since the atmosphere is at a slight pressure, and since the earth has its own magnetic field (though a weak one), any Xenon in the atmosphere would automatically create the energy we have been discussing. The energy is in many ways like light, though it is extremely penetrating and can pass readily through any substance.

For the benefit of scientists who may chance to read this book, we would point out that a very powerful beam of Xenon energy — and consequently a greater degree of healing power — can be obtained by deliberately collecting a quantity of pure Xenon in a non-magnetic container, under a pressure of at least 300 psi and by placing it within a magnetic field of at least 200 Gauss. Twice-weekly exposures of damaged locations of the body to the energy field thus produced, for about 30 minutes at a time, will in most cases be sufficient to allow the body to begin a rapid program of tissue reconstruction.

We have detoured from our main theme in this chapter for the purpose of explaining certain ideas regarding the body's ability to rebuild its own tissue. But now we wish to return to the concept of death, to show you that it is entirely an illusion, and that nothing of the true essence of the individual is lost at death.

When you die you merely lay aside the physical cloak which you put on at birth, just as was done by the little bird you found by the side of the path that day in the woods. You have another body — the astral one — to which your conscious mind immediately switches. As far as the conscious mind is concerned, there is hardly any difference between the two bodies, and in many cases a person who has just died does not know or believe that he is "dead". The feeling of being alive is just as strong as before the laying aside of the physical cloak. It is even somewhat amusing to watch the efforts of some who have just passed out of physical life, as they strain to make themselves seen or heard by those who remain. In most such cases, of course, it is impossible, and eventually the 'dead' individual gives up the attempt and accepts that something is definitely 'different' about his status, even though he feels exactly the same as before.

When an individual who has died comes to accept his new status (many do this right away), he can be contacted and taken to the astral plane that is most suited to the next phase of his experience. The astral planes are merely locations where the astral body is 'at home', so to speak. For the most part, these are happy levels where souls are encouraged to drop all their old pretenses and inhibitions, and to 'work off' any difficult habits of thought, emotion or action they might have acquired while living on the earth. For example, if a person has lived a life as a housewife but has always wanted to become a famous writer, she will be given an opportunity to realize her wish in the astral plane. The purpose of such an arrangement is not actually to train her as a writer, but to allow her to get *rid* of the intense desire to be something she was not.

Such a strong wish can be an impediment to further soul-progress, and the purpose of the astral sojourn is to allow these impediments to fall away. After a certain time devoted to developing the skills of a writer, the individual will eventually get her fill of that kind of experience, and will be ready for something else. At that point she will be clear of the strong desire that bound her to the earth plane, and she will be ready for the next level of her between-life experience.

This next level is normally one at a higher plane of being, where she will come into contact with the guides and angels who have helped her through all of her lives, arranging the patterns of existence so that she can learn the maximum in each incarnation, and can set aside as much Karma as possible. She will discuss with them the best future earth-life for herself, the kinds of lessons she might still have to work on, and the best way to lift more of the karmic burden which she has yet to discharge. When a decision is made as to the next life experience, preparations will be made to tie her to a new physical body, and this will take place at about the time that the new body takes its first breath at birth.

What we have explained here is much simplified. A broader and more detailed discussion is given in our earlier book, *Seasons of the Spirit,* and we hope one day that you will wish to read that book as well. But for now, the ideas just dealt with will suffice.

One area, however, should be discussed in greater detail. This area has to do with the very process by which the new body is formed in the womb of the mother. Normally, when it has been decided which soul is to inhabit the new body that is forming in the womb, the energies of that soul are tapped to help in the growth process for the foetus. The soul-energies are of different kinds, and each one is best suited to promote the growth of certain organs which are closest to it in quality or 'vibration'. For example, you know that you have an emotional/love side to your nature. This side partakes of what we call the heart facet of the soul. The energies produced from this part of the soul are those used to build the structure of the heart organ itself.

When the amount of heart-energy available from the soul is insufficient, the structure of the heart is perturbed or weakened in some way, and the result is that the body which is inhabited by the soul is below par in the exact same sense as the soul. In other words, a soul who is deficient in heart energy will inhabit a body that has a weakened or debilitated heart structure. In this way it is hoped that there will be a constant reminder, at least at the subconscious level, that the soul requires some additional balancing or improvement in the heart/love energies. Since these energies are those which fuel the feelings of friendship and affection, and since the development of this facet of the human being is of paramount importance, you can see the value of holding up this constant reminder before the inner sight of the individual.

Precisely the same correspondence between the physical body and the qualities of the soul takes place for all the major organs, although the details of this relationship are too complex for us to deal with here. What we would ask you to remember is that the physical body is one of the best examples of *reality as a mirror,* although the aspects which the body mirrors are the higher qualities of the soul.

In the next chapter we will discuss in greater detail the ways in which *all* of your life-pattern acts as a mirror, telling you things about yourself, pointing out connections and meanings that your conscious mind may have overlooked, and reminding you that you are not alone and abandoned upon the earth.

Chapter 12

Symbolism, Sexuality and Love

The ways of reality are wondrous, and would be seen as such if only man could allow himself to believe that *everything has meaning*. The lines in your palm, the shape of your nose, the structure of your heart — all these have something to say about the real you, the you that is eternal. But around you too are events and circumstances that have significance.

For example, if you try to telephone a friend and find that she is out, or that the line is always busy, you are being given a signal that such a contact is not right just then. Reality is saying to you: 'don't waste your time in this direction; move on to something else; leave it for another time.'

Many people refuse to see any significance in the clues which reality hands them constantly. They keep on banging their heads against closed doors, thinking that sheer force will get them what they want. But those who read the signals from their life-pattern find that the world goes much more smoothly. Any who can believe that virtually every event in their lives is telling them things at some other level can learn to live in harmony with life. Happiness will be the inevitable result.

Let us give you another example. Suppose that a person is driving too fast and is stopped by the police for speeding. Now, most people would merely think that they had run into a piece of bad luck, would complain to themselves for a while, and then would forget the incident. But the person who knows how to read the signals in his life would know right away that this event was saying to him that there was something *else* in his life that he was trying to move ahead too fast, that he was 'speeding' in some other area of his experience, and not merely at the level of car-driving. Such a person can then re-assess what he is trying to do at the other level, and perhaps make a change which will be beneficial.

There are so many examples of this sort that it would waste the available space to list them. But we think you can see the sort of approach that should be taken to the apparently 'chance' events in life: that approach is to assume that they are not chance at all, and that they were arranged to fall across your path for a reason — namely to *tell* you something.

In our book, *Symbols*, there are many examples of the ways that reality talks continuously to each incarnated soul. One day, we hope that you will read that book.

Before moving on to the last chapter, we must deal with one area which will demand more from your understanding than the topics we have already discussed. That area relates to the sexual side of experience. You are only now reaching the age when your sexuality can awaken, and we hope the ideas we are going to deal with here will allow that flowering to take place in the most beautiful and joyous way possible.

There are many people upon the earth who are terribly confused about the idea of sex. Some see it as mainly a selfish pursuit, to be indulged for one's own pleasure alone. Others think it is somehow 'dirty' or 'nasty', and are secretly ashamed of the drives they feel within themselves. Still others are caught up in the idea that the passionate or sexual side of affection is the only real aspect it has, and they do not allow themselves to experience pure love for another person without the distraction that the sexual nature causes.

Love is many-sided. It can be expressed in the mental plane — through words or through writing; it can be expressed through the emotions — by the feeling of affection and love for another; and it can be expressed at the physical level — through a hug, or a kiss on the cheek, or in the sexual embrace itself. Because man has all three of these facets to his nature, his love-experience is only complete when *all three* sides are present. This does *not* require that there be a sexual side to all of his relationships, by any means, because the sexual act is only one of many ways that the body can be used to express the affectional urges. But for love to manifest fully, there needs to be some token of it at all three levels. A relationship purely at the emotional level, and without some mental interchange, ceases after a time to be stimulating. Likewise an affair that is primarily physical in nature, with little true affection felt, eventually palls and dies. It is the same for any combination that does not partake of all three facets which make up the race of man.

What we are saying, then, is that it is of supreme importance to keep the interchange between a man and a woman functioning at all three levels of the triangle: mental, emotional and physical. Of course, in your own case there can be no complete sexual experience for a number of years. But do not neglect the necessity of developing a *demonstrative* side to your affection. When you are fond of somebody, hug them, or give them a kiss on the cheek. And don't neglect the mental facet either. People need to be told you are fond of them or that you love them. There is a power in the spoken word 'love' that you cannot possibly imagine. It literally unlocks the hidden chambers of a closed heart, and makes spring bloom in the soul.

Above all, allow your heart to *feel* the emotion of love whenever you sense the little tug that signifies it is near. Love is not just for a boyfriend, or for a parent. Every soul incarnate on the earth is worthy of your love. You need only allow it through, and your heart will be swept away on a tide of affection.

Many think that they cannot control the love-ability in their hearts. They think that the heart dictates and they merely follow. But like every human quality, love too can be made to respond to the will. You can literally *decide* that you are going to love a particular person, and you will be able to do it. This is what Christ was implying when he told his listeners that they should love their enemies. They were incredulous, of course, and could not understand that the loving process was under their control if they willed it to be.

If you would but practice loving, you would make yourself into a fountain of healing energy where your brothers could drink the balm that heals the pain of the soul. For it is love, only love, that can heal at *all* levels of the human being — whether the physical, the astral, the aetheric or the soul itself.

One final thing: remember that the earth being also needs your love. Many give lip-service to the notion of the earth as a living creature, and do not realize that it is literally true in the most real sense. Not only is the earth a living, thinking, feeling entity like yourself, but she needs the love and the thoughts of the human race in these darkening years as she has never before needed anything. She feels alone. She feels as if man has abandoned her. He scars her beautiful mantle and explodes devastating bombs under her surface. He pollutes her atmosphere with his chemicals and his hatred. Is it any wonder that she feels alone?

You can be among the few who realize that the mother planet of the race is suffering, and you can act to relieve that suffering. In your prayers, and in your meditation, send her your love and your thoughts. She knows when any think of her with affection, and the darkness of her days can be lifted by the love of the race she has nurtured since its inception.

In the following and last chapter of this book, we wish to address the readers of this book directly, for we have a message that we hope will change the path of many of your brothers into one of love, uplift and joy. Unless millions of human beings can come, as you have, to a new and higher understanding of their purpose upon this earth, there is little hope that the darkness of the present time can be removed.

Chapter 13

The Message

You are a child of the Living God, even as are the angels, the planets and suns of the Cosmos, or the tiniest flower that perches upon a wind-whipped rock. For each of His creations, the All in All has an abundance of love so vast that no human conception could ever encompass it.

To you He has given a fragment of His Mind so that you could reason and think, a part of His Divine Love so that you could return to Him at least a faint reflection of the all-embracing and all-forgiving affection which He floods upon each of His creatures, and finally the right to create, from His Body, a body of your own.

In creating your body, you have followed minutely the patterns which exist at the level of your higher self. Every flaw in your physical form is a reflection of a flaw in your soul. It is the hope — it is your hope, whether you would recognize it or not — that the experience of a body flawed in such a symbolic way will encourage you to make the effort required to correct the flaws that are found in your higher part.

You have come to the earth plane knowing full well that it is a mirror for your own thoughts, feelings and actions. You understand at your deepest levels that what surrounds you in terms of the circumstances of your life is merely the reflected mirror image of the states of being which are found within yourself.

You have also come in order to lighten the load of karma which your soul carries, knowing that each illness, each emotional hurt, each mental wound, is setting aside an old debt that you yourself have erected, that you literally owe to yourself.

In your progress through the vast eons of time upon this beautiful planet, you have trod many by-ways. At times you have risen to giddy peaks of spiritual awareness and achievement. At others you have sunk into the morass of sin, and tasted all of the ungodliest experiences that the earth makes available.

But through it all, your soul has held firmly to its goal: to succeed in its quest for spiritual light, to cleanse itself of the negative habits and traits accumulated through many lifetimes, and to be rid at last of the heavy burden of karmic consequence which it carries, like Pilgrim in the book, as evidence that it has strayed from the perfection of the Creator's laws.

The fact that this book has fallen into your hands has been no mere chance accident. The Guides and Helpers who love you and who always will, have gone to great pains to ensure that your conscious mind is presented with the ideas and concepts which this book embodies. Indeed, little in your life has arisen through blind happenstance. All of life upon this earth is planned as minutely as possible, in order that no possibility of helping mankind is neglected.

In the months and years ahead of you, there will come opportunities to help others, and opportunities to learn that which uplifts the spirit. Do not turn from these chances, for they will never come again in just the same way. For many readers of this book, these opportunities may be the last they will ever be given. We are not indulging in idle threats when we say that many souls now upon this earth are literally at the *last* fork in the road that can ever be presented to them. If they make the choice which is against the Creator's laws, then they are, in every sense of the word, lost. The opportunity will never come again.

Remember always that the outcome of your life is in

your hands. No salvation can ever be purchased by the suffering of another. Christ's death on Calvary was to symbolize your right to try again to do what you have failed at in the past. But *you* must do it; *you* must scale the mountain of spiritual acheivement by your own strength; *you* must reach out to God — for even though He holds His arms out always to you, that by itself is not enough to save you from your own evil.

Finally, remember that the universe was created for Love. The God of All that Is wished to make souls so that He could feel His Divine Love more keenly. This can only fully occur when His creatures *return* that love to Him, to the maximum level of which they are capable.

All of the souls and entities at the level from which this dictation is originating feel deeply the distress of their human brothers at this hour, as the shadows of the Great Trial lengthen upon the planet. We know what tests lie just ahead; we know the risks that are to be run; we know the sorrow and pain that must visit the race.

We send you our love, our thoughts, our strength. Ask to benefit from these vibrations being flooded into the earth, and you shall. It matters not whether you address your prayer to your angel, to Jesus, to God, or to any other entity. All creatures great and small are emanations from the One Creator. When you ask any being for help, God knows you are asking Him.

Stand firm in what you yourself believe. Hold to your own conviction of the truth above any other source, whether it be psychics, mediums, scriptures, or this very book. The truth that is *your* truth is written in the scrolls of your heart, for there too abides the Living God. Seek only to *live* that truth, to hold your own light high so that those who grope in darkness may see, and to tread the path that you believe your life has set before you.

If you remain true to yourself, if you believe in the right, and if you place your hand into the hand of God, then no evil, no lasting sorrow, and no permanent pain will ever befall you.

May the peace and blessing of all the higher beings who care for humanity's struggle be with you forevermore.

OM MANI PADME HUM

Hilarion Mailing List

If you wish to be kept informed regarding Workshops in the Hilarion material, speaking tours by Maurice B. Cooke, and our regular special offers of new books and cassette tapes at reduced prices, please write to us at the address below and we will be happy to include your name on our regular mailing list.

Marcus Books
195 Randolph Rd.,
Toronto, Canada, M4G 3S6